Useful Machines

Wheels

Chris Oxlade

Heinemann Library
Chicago, Illinois

Customer Service   888–454–2279

Visit our website at www.heinemannlibrary.com

Originated by Ambassador Litho Ltd.
Printed and bound in China by South China Printing Company

07 06 05 04 03
10 9 8 7 6 5 4 3 2 1

Library of Congress Cataloging-in-Publication Data
Oxlade, Chris.
  Wheels / Chris Oxlade.
      p. cm. -- (Useful machines)
Includes bibliographical references and index.
Summary: Describes what wheels are and how they work, different types of wheels and their uses, and other facts about wheels.
  ISBN 1-4034-3665-7 (lib. bdg.) -- ISBN 1-4034-3680-0 (pbk.)
  1. Simple machines--Juvenile literature. 2. Wheels--Juvenile literature. [1. Wheels.] I. Title. II. Series.
  TJ147.O89 2003
  621.8--dc21
                            2003003790

Acknowledgments
The author and publisher are grateful to the following for permission to reproduce copyright material:
pp. 4, 14 SPL; p. 5 Comstock Images; pp. 6, 21, 22, 27 Alamy Images; pp. 7, 9, 11 Peter Morris; p. 8 Jens Haas/Corbis; p. 10 David H. Wells/Corbis; pp. 12, 25 Imagebank; p. 13 Robert Clare/Taxi; p. 15 Pictor Uniphoto; p. 16 Duomo/Corbis; p. 17 Giles Chapman; p. 18 James A. Sugar/Corbis; pp. 19, 20 Getty Images; p. 23 J. Greenburg/Trip; p. 24 Corbis/Royalty-Free; p. 26 Robert Estall/Corbis; p. 29 Lester Lefkowitz/Corbis.

Cover photograph by Imagebank.

Some words are shown in bold, **like this.** You can find out what they mean by looking in the glossary.

Contents

What Is a Wheel?

A machine makes our lives easier by helping us do things. Machines are made up of **simple machines** that work together. A wheel is a simple machine.

A wheel is a very useful machine. This stroller has three wheels. The wheels make it easy to move the stroller forward and backward.

What Does a Wheel Do?

Most wheels are found on cars, bicycles, inline skates, and other things that move along the ground. Wheels make it easier for these things to move.

CD
TUNER
DVD
AUX
MD / TAPE
VOLUME

Wheels can also change the size of a movement. This is a stereo volume control knob. It is **attached** to a **shaft** on the inside. When you turn the knob, the **shaft** only turns a little.

7

Parts of a Wheel

spokes

A wheel is a round, flat object. Solid wheels do not have any holes in them. Other wheels have many parts. They may have **spokes.** Spokes make bicycle wheels much lighter than solid wheels.

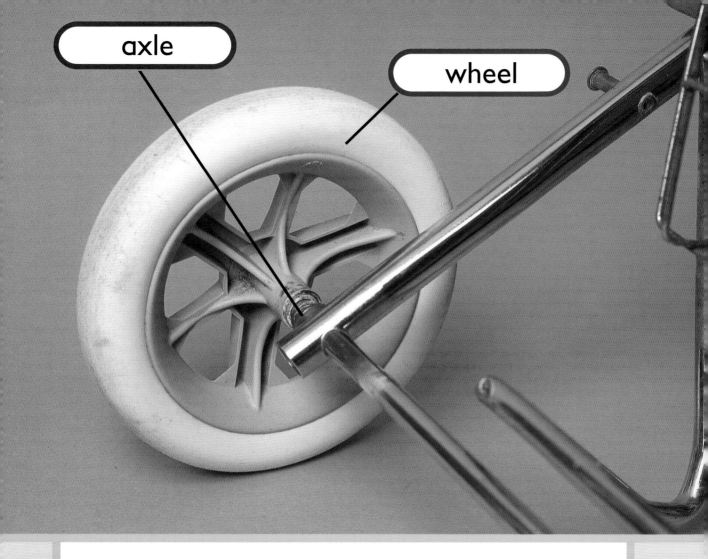

axle

wheel

The center of a wheel is always **attached** to a rod called an **axle.** Some axles turn when the wheel turns. Other axles do not turn with the wheel.

How a Wheel Works

Heavy things are hard to slide along the ground. A **force** called **friction** keeps them from moving easily. Wheels cut down on friction.

Wheels can also make movements bigger or smaller. A doorknob works like a wheel. When you turn the doorknob, it makes a small **push** or **pull** on the door **latch.**

Wheels for Moving

Wheels help things move along the ground more easily. A skateboard has four tough rubber wheels. The wheels turn on the ground as the skateboard moves.

Most wheelchairs have two big wheels at the back and two small wheels at the front. The person in the wheelchair **pushes** on the rims of the big wheels to make the wheelchair move.

Wheels for Transportation

Motorcycles, cars, buses, and trucks all have wheels. The wheels let these heavy **vehicles** move along the road. Rubber tires give a smooth ride. They also keep the wheels from slipping.

Trains carry very heavy **loads.**
Their wheels run on smooth metal
tracks. This cuts down on **friction.**
Train wheels need to be very strong.
They are made from solid steel.

Making Wheels Turn

This boy is pressing on the pedals of a tricycle. This makes the front wheel turn. The wheel **pushes** against the ground. The tricycle moves forward.

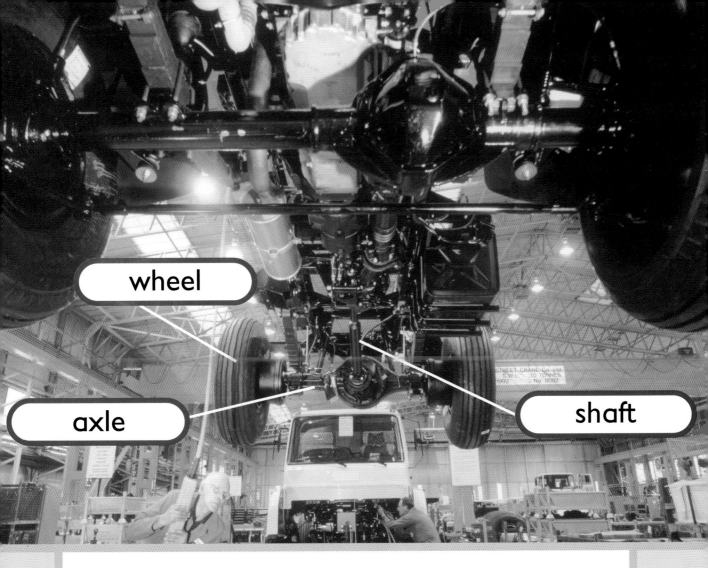

wheel

axle

shaft

Cars, buses, and trucks have **engines.**
This truck's engine turns a rod called a
shaft. The shaft spins the back wheels.
The wheels push against the road. This
makes the truck move.

Wheels for Rolling

Some wheels are not used for moving other things. This rolling pin rolls along the **dough** when you **push** it. This flattens the dough.

This box is moving along a roller table. The top of the table has a lot of wheels. The wheels spin under the box. This helps it slide along easily.

More Useful Wheels

Trucks and buses have big **steering** wheels. The steering wheel turns a **shaft attached** to the wheels on the ground. The shaft turns the wheels to the left or the right.

wheel

Here is a wheel for turning a garden hose on and off. The wheel turns a rod that goes into the pipe. Turning the rod without the wheel would be very hard to do.

Wheels in Machines

Many machines have wheels that help them work. This crane has many **pulley** wheels. They help it lift heavy **loads.**

This machine measures lengths. The person **pushes** the machine along the ground. This makes the wheel turn. Each time the wheel turns once, it means the person has walked three feet (one meter).

Gear Wheels

A **gear wheel** is a special kind of wheel. It has teeth all the way around its edge. Many machines have gear wheels inside of them.

Gear wheels work together. They are put next to each other so that their teeth meet up. When one wheel turns, the other wheel turns, too.

Gear Wheels in Machines

These huge **gear wheels** are inside a windmill. The gear wheels move other parts of the windmill. The windmill grinds wheat and other grains.

Some gear wheels are very small. These gear wheels are inside a wristwatch. They make the hands of the watch turn at the right speed.

Amazing Wheel Facts

- The wheel is one of the oldest machines in the world. It was invented more than 5,000 years ago.
- On old sailing ships, the heavy **anchor** was **pulled** up by a huge wheel called a capstan wheel.
- Before wheels were invented, people moved heavy stones by using logs to roll them along the ground.
- The smallest **gear wheels** ever made are thinner than a hair from your head. They were made just to see how small we could make them.

The wheels of this dump truck are much taller than a person. This kind of huge dump truck is used in a mine.

Glossary

anchor   heavy object that keeps a boat from moving

attach   fasten or join together

axle   rod that attaches to the center of a wheel

dough   mix that is used to make bread

engine   machine that turns energy into movement

force   push or pull

friction   force that slows down moving objects

gear wheel   wheel with teeth around its edge

latch   metal part that keeps a door closed

load   amount of weight that you are trying to move

pull   move something closer to you

pulley   simple machine that makes lifting or pulling objects easier

push   move something away from you

shaft   rod that spins around

simple machine   machine with no moving parts

spoke   rod that connects the center of a wheel to the outside of a wheel

steer   make a vehicle or a boat change direction

vehicle   machine that carries people or things from place to place

More Books to Read

Douglas, Lloyd G. *What Is a Wheel and Axle?* Danbury, Conn.: Scholastic Library Publishing, 2002.

Pipe, Jim. *What Does a Wheel Do?: Projects about Rolling and Sliding.* Brookfield, Conn.: Millbrook Press, 2002.

Welsbacher, Anne. *Wheels and Axles.* Minnetonka, Minn.: Capstone Press, 2000.

Index